MAR 14

THE MAN WHO INVENTED THE LASER

The Genius of Theodore H. Maiman

Titles in the *Genius Inventors and Their Great Ideas* Series:

GENIUS INVENTORS AND THEIR GREAT IDEAS

THE MAN WHO INVENTED THE LASER

The Genius of Theodore H. Maiman

Edwin Brit Wyckoff

Enslow Elementary

an imprint of

Enslow Publishers, Inc.
40 Industrial Road
Box 398
Berkeley Heights, NJ 07922
USA

http://www.enslow.com

Content Advisor
Andrew H. Rawicz
Professor of Engineering
Simon Fraser University
Vancouver, Canada

Series Literacy Consultant
Allan A. De Fina, Ph.D.
Past President of the New Jersey Reading Association
Professor, Department of Literacy Education
New Jersey City University

Enslow Elementary, an imprint of Enslow Publishers, Inc.

Enslow Elementary® is a registered trademark of Enslow Publishers, Inc.

Acknowledgment

The publisher thanks Theodore and Kathleen Maiman for providing many helpful suggestions and photos for the publication of this book.

Library of Congress Cataloging-in-Publication Data

Wyckoff, Edwin Brit.
  The man who invented the laser: the genius of Theodore H. Maiman/Edwin Brit Wyckoff.
    p. cm. — (Genius inventors and their great ideas)
  Includes bibliographical references and index.
  ISBN 978-0-7660-4138-7 (alk. paper)
  1. Maiman, Theodore H.—Juvenile literature. 2. Physicists—United States—Biography—Juvenile literature.
  3. Lasers—History—Juvenile literature. I. Title.
  QC16.M334W93 2013
  621.36'6092—dc23
  [B]
                                        2012013979

Future editions:
Paperback ISBN: 978-1-4644-0208-1
Single-User PDF ISBN: 978-0-7660-1121-6

EPUB ISBN: 978-1-4645-1121-9
Multi-User PDF ISBN: 978-0-7660-5750-0

Printed in the United States of America.
032013 Lake Book Manufacturing, Inc., Melrose Park, IL
10 9 8 7 6 5 4 3 2 1

To Our Readers: We have done our best to make sure all Internet addresses in this book were active and appropriate when we went to press. However, the author and the publisher have no control over and assume no liability for the material available on those Internet sites or on other Web sites they may link to. Any comments or suggestions can be sent by e-mail to comments@enslow.com or to the address on the back cover.

♻ Enslow Publishers, Inc., is committed to printing our books on recycled paper. The paper in every book contains 10% to 30% post-consumer waste (PCW). The cover board on the outside of each book contains 100% PCW. Our goal is to do our part to help young people and the environment too!

Photo Credits: AIP Emilio Segre Visual Archives, Hecht Collection, p. 21; Courtesy Air Force Laboratory's Directed Energy Directorate, p. 5 (top); Courtesy HRL Labratories, LLC, pp. 22, 24, 26; Courtesy Kathleen Maiman, pp. 9, 11, 17, 25, 27, 28, 30, 37; Courtesy of the Maiman Family, p. 15; Courtesy Robin M. Izzo, p. 8; Courtesy University of Colorado Alumni Association pp, 1, 5 (bottom); Homer and Jean Hill, p. 12; ©iStockphoto.com/Jason Verschoor p. 33; NASA/JPL, p. 6; Sam Ogden/Photo Researchers, Inc., p. 35; Shutterstock.com, pp. 19, 39, 41, 42, 47.

Cover Photo: Theodore Maiman: Courtesy University of Colorado Alumni Association; Laser: Shutterstock

CONTENTS

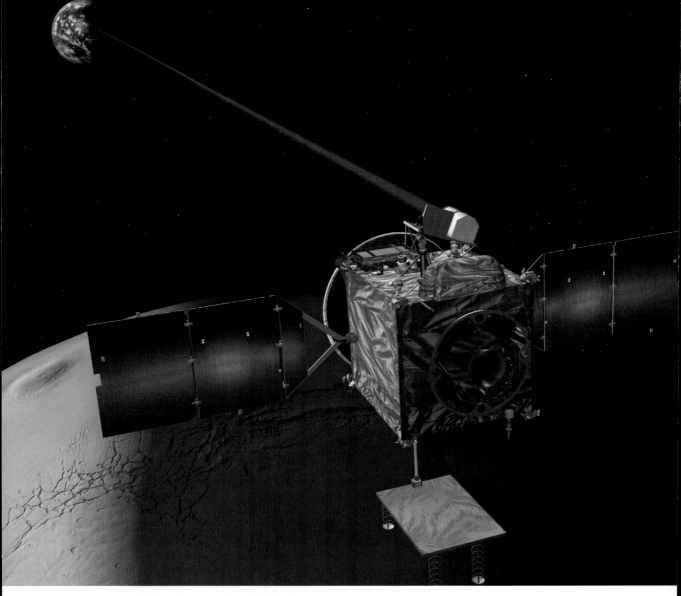

This picture was created by a computer. It shows how a beam of light could travel from Earth to a spacecraft. In space, the beam would be invisible.

Chapter 1

The Unstoppable Boy

A very narrow beam of light was sent racing into the sky from the United States in 2005. It was testing contact between Earth and MESSENGER, a U.S spacecraft exploring other planets. The narrow rays of light were aimed at a mirror on the ship only six inches wide. They bounced back 15 million miles to Earth at blazing speeds. Amazingly, the beam of light came from a lamp using only about thirty watts of power. That is no stronger than the light bulb inside an ordinary oven in an ordinary home. This light was not movie magic. It was a laser.

Lasers make very narrow, very bright beams of light. Today there are many kinds of lasers made from many different materials. Doctors can use one kind of laser like a

TWO KINDS OF LIGHT

Light from a regular bulb spreads in every direction.

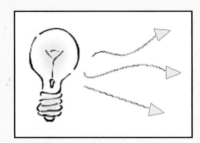

It is very hard to read with only a ten-watt bulb.

Light from a laser is very narrow, very concentrated, and very powerful.

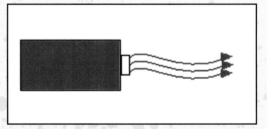

A ten-watt light in a laser shoots out a very narrow beam. To make a laser, light is bounced back and forth inside a material such as ruby. With each bounce, the light gets stronger until it escapes out of one side as a laser beam.

Ted Maiman and his sister, Estelle

knife to operate on delicate human eyes. Other kinds of laser beams carry so much energy they can cut through thick steel.

Many scientists worked on the idea of lasers in the 1950s. But no one knew how to make laser light. Ted Maiman had his own ideas about lasers. Almost every scientist he talked to said that his ideas would not work. But Ted did not listen. He would not give up trying to build his laser.

Theodore Harold Maiman was born in Los Angeles, California, on July 11, 1927. The next year, he moved to Denver, Colorado with his parents, Abe and Rose Ann, and his sister Estelle. They lived in one big building with grandparents, aunts, and uncles.

Ted wanted to know how everything worked. His family had great patience as he took apart every machine he could get his hands on. When he was three, he insisted that the light in the refrigerator stayed on even when the door was closed. His mother cleaned out all the food and let Ted climb inside while she stood guard. The light stayed on all the time because the switch was not working. She let her little genius out and had the light switch fixed. Another time, Ted decided that all his aunt's pretty lipsticks, creams, and face powder were really for mixing up into great new colors. Even a loving aunt did not think that was funny.

Ted was full of energy and curiosity. He became the class clown, making all his classmates laugh. One teacher

Ted with his parents, Abe and Rose Ann

decided to try to calm him down. She gave him special math problems to solve. He liked that.

Ted enjoyed his busy life. He went to clarinet practice with the high school band at seven in the morning. After school, he rushed downtown to his job in a shop that fixed broken radios. Then he raced back home for dinner.

Ted moved to Morristown, New Jersey, when he was sixteen.

Afterward, Ted hurried back downtown to the University of Colorado to take a free class on how radios work. He was only about twelve years old.

In 1939 the United States was getting ready for World War II. Ted's boss decided to work in a factory making equipment for soldiers. He surprised Ted by offering to let him run the shop all by himself. Ted, at age thirteen, took charge. His family moved to Morrristown, New Jersey in 1943, which ended his career as a radio repairman.

Chapter 2

The Attic Laboratory

Ted's father, Abe, was a very good electronics engineer. He invented a system that helped radios work off the electrical batteries in cars. He also thought up a new way to let doctors hear a human heartbeat much more clearly. Abe hoped that Ted would grow up to make things that would help doctors save lives. He put together a laboratory in the attic of their home in Morristown. At night and on weekends, Abe worked on his inventions. Ted watched and listened. Soon, he began trying his own experiments.

Ted built a strong magnet powered by electricity. He set it up right next to one of his father's delicate scientific tools. When he turned on the magnet, it tore his father's

As a teen, Ted learned much about electronics.

tool to pieces. Abe said nothing, but for years Ted still felt very bad about it.

Ted was in high school when he got a job moving heavy electrical machinery in a factory. The work was backbreaking. The pay was sixty cents an hour. He asked for a different job. He wanted to work with electrical wires, which paid ninety cents an hour. The owners said no to the sixteen-year-old. Even so, Ted never stopped asking for better jobs. One year later, he was building parts for radios for the war. World War II was still raging in Europe and Asia.

Ted turned seventeen in 1944. It was time to join the United States Navy. There he would work on signaling equipment.

Ted in his navy uniform

Chapter 3

Mastering Physics

After serving in the navy, Ted entered the University of Colorado to study science. In 1949, he graduated with a degree in engineering physics. But his heart was still set on studying physics. Physics would help him understand computers, television, and even ideas about lasers. The famous Stanford University in California did not accept him. So he traveled to New York City to study physics at Columbia University.

But Ted was stubborn. He applied to Stanford University again and again. He was sure it would be the best school for him. The university said no every time. Then he asked to study engineering instead of physics. This time,

Engineers use math and physics to design and build new things like cars, computers, airplanes, cameras, and musical instruments.

he was told yes. In 1951, he earned a master's degree in electrical engineering. With this degree, and after years of being told no, Ted was finally able to study advanced physics at Stanford.

At the university, Ted worked as a laboratory assistant for Dr. Willis Lamb, who would later win a Nobel Prize for physics. Ted's work was so good that Dr. Lamb wanted Ted to stay longer and longer. But Ted wanted to finish his studies and move on with his own work.

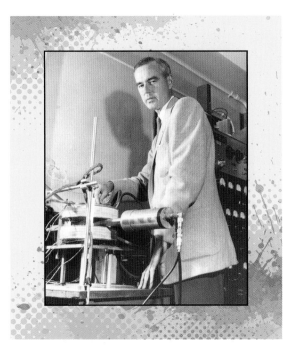

Dr. Willis Lamb won the Nobel Prize in Physics in 1955. The Nobel Prize is one of the world's highest honors for a scientist.

Ted made a deal with Dr. Lamb. Before he would graduate from Stanford, Ted would train a bright

Irwin Wieder (right) learned many of the same ideas about physics as Ted in Dr. Lamb's laboratory.

young man named Irwin Wieder to take over his job. Ted earned his doctorate in physics in 1955.

Free at last, it was time for a vacation. Ted wanted to travel. He bought a ticket for a boat trip around the world. He had gone only halfway when he decided the vacation was over. He wanted to start working. He flew back to

California on the first flight he could get. In January of 1956, Ted quickly found a job at the Hughes Research Laboratory in Culver City.

Ted settled down and married Shirley Rich that year. In 1958 their daughter, Sheri, was born. Life on the California coast was pleasant, but soon it would all change.

The Hughes Research Laboratory is known as HRL Laboratories today. This picture shows the lab in Malibu, California. It moved there in 1960.

Chapter 4

The Laser Light Mystery

In 1959, Hughes Research Laboratory put Ted in charge of a project to build a laser. Many scientists said that it could not be done. Other scientists said that a laser could not do anything useful. Ted just closed his ears and began working on lasers.

Hughes Research Laboratory gave him $50,000 to pay one assistant and to buy equipment. That sounds like a lot of money. It was not. Research teams at other companies had hundreds of scientists and millions of dollars to spend. The lasers those teams wanted to build were huge and had to be cooled way down below freezing.

Ted had different ideas about his laser. First, he wanted his laser to work at room temperature. Second, his

Ted with one of his lasers

laser had to be small enough to hold in his hand. Nobody could change his mind.

Ted had some dark red rubies left over from his early experiments at the university. But sending beams of light through them didn't work very well. So, he used a pink

Ted's first laser was small enough to hold in his hand.

ruby. He tried and tried to make laser light. But nothing happened. Most other laser scientists thought Ted's idea would not work, because they were trying to use clouds of chemical gas.

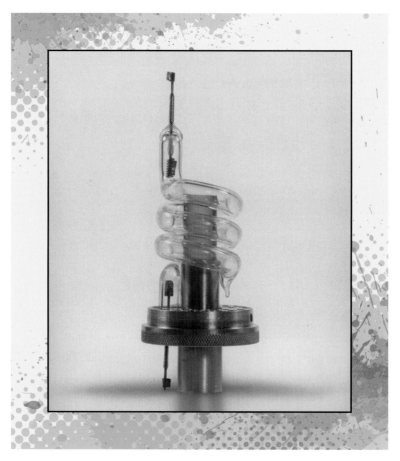

The first laser

Then the young scientist Ted had trained at Stanford, Irwin Wieder, did tests on pink rubies. The tests showed they would never make laser light. Ted would not listen to other scientists, but he believed Wieder because he had trained him himself. Racing against time, Ted gave up on the ruby and tried using many other kinds of materials.

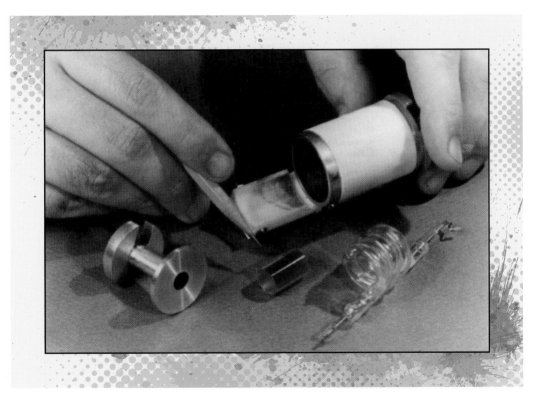

This is the pink ruby and the lamp used in the first laser.

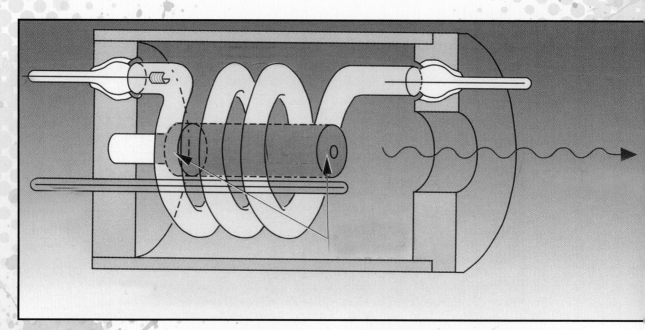

This drawing shows how the first laser worked. When the light tube was lit up, light bounced back and forth inside the ruby. As it bounced, it got stronger until it escaped as a laser beam.

The $50,000 began to drain away. Ted put in long hours at the laboratory. He took work home, just the way his father had done. Shirley hated the loneliness and the pressure. She and Ted would later divorce. The endless search for the perfect laser design had taken over their lives.

Ted was never willing to take anything for granted. Just because some famous scientists thought rubies would not work, they did not convince him. He decided to check Wieder's tests. This time, the tests showed the ruby could make laser light. Wieder and all the other scientists had been wrong. Even the smartest people can make mistakes.

Ted turned back to the pink ruby. He ordered a new one about the size of a sugar cube. He sent away for a photographic lamp that sent out sharp, powerful flashes of light. Waiting for the ruby and the lamp to be shipped to him seemed to take forever. It was April of 1960. Eight months passed since he had started his research, and there was still no laser. Most of the money had been spent.

Ted holds the first laser. Behind him is the much larger Nova laser at the Lawrence Livermore National Laboratory in Livermore, California.

The next month, the special lamp and the new pink ruby arrived. Ted and his assistant put together a little device that could be held in one hand. They turned on the power. A very narrow, brilliant light burned through the air. The laser light mystery had been solved. Ted Maiman had invented and built the first laser.

An important science writer called Ted's laser a fake. Newspaper headlines shouted that a "death ray" had been invented. That was silly. Angry scientists said again and again that the laser was an invention that could not do anything. They would be proved wrong. Ted knew that he had created something useful.

Chapter 5

Listening to Himself

Many people spend their lives playing follow the leader. Even scientists may be afraid to break the rules somebody famous laid down years before. The rules for a laser that most scientists were following never included a small pink ruby. That may be why it took so long to build the first laser.

Inventors like Ted Maiman go to work every day trying to make their ideas work, but many things do not work right the first time. They stay awake at night trying to figure out how to fix what went wrong. It is like trying to finish a jigsaw puzzle without a picture to use as a guide. Many people give up just before they could have put the whole puzzle together. One extra

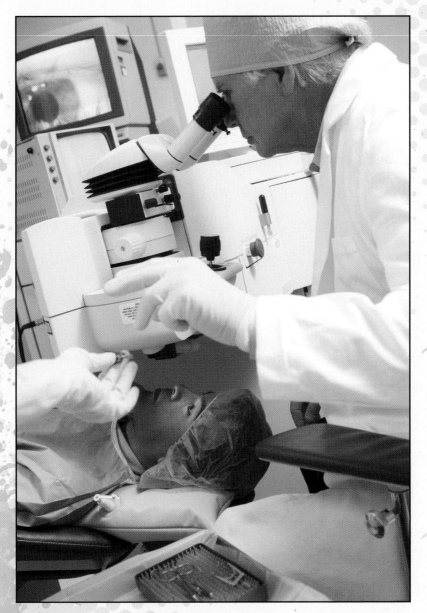

Lasers today can be used in eye surgery.

drop of courage keeps inventors going when everyone else has given up.

Abe Maiman lived to see his son win science prizes from all around the world for his fantastic invention. He remembered spending time with young Ted in his attic laboratory. Abe had wanted his son to use physics and engineering to help doctors help people. He saw his son's lasers used by doctors for difficult surgery. Today, lasers repair human eyes thousands of times every year. They help destroy cancer in many patients.

In 1984, Ted was voted to become a member of America's National Inventors Hall of Fame. Awards kept pouring in as new uses for lasers were discovered. He married again. He and his wife, Kathleen, lived in Vancouver, Canada, until his death in May 2007.

Ted Maiman had the extra drop of courage to listen to himself when everyone else told him he was wrong. He has the delicious, delightful, wonderful memory of having been right all along.

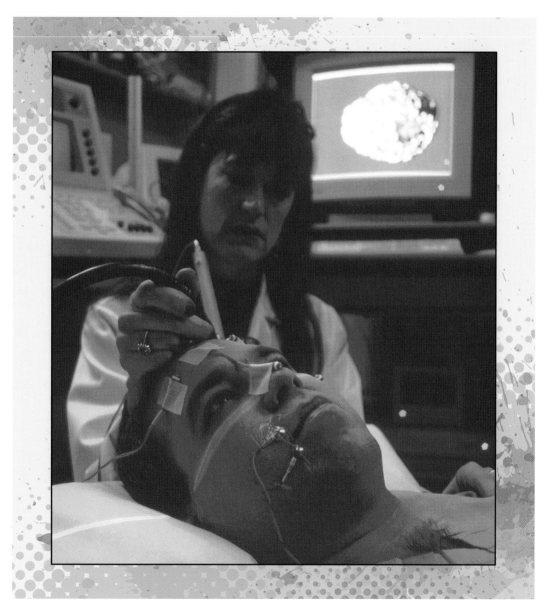

A laser helps to map this man's brain.

LASERS CAN DO FANTASTIC THINGS

The brilliant light from lasers can be sharper than a knife and hotter than a blowtorch. These are just a few things lasers can do:

- Create fabulous light shows for theaters and music concerts
- Cut steel and other metals
- Weld metal together
- Burn holes through metal
- Burn holes in diamonds
- Handle delicate eye surgery
- Remove tattoos
- Eliminate birthmarks
- Help surgeons operate without causing bleeding
- Read laserdiscs, CDs, and DVDs
- Send phone calls through a fiberglass strand thinner than human hair
- Measure the distance from the Earth to the Moon
- Guide airplanes and spacecraft
- Read the price barcode with a supermarket scanner
- Cut stacks of cloth to make clothing

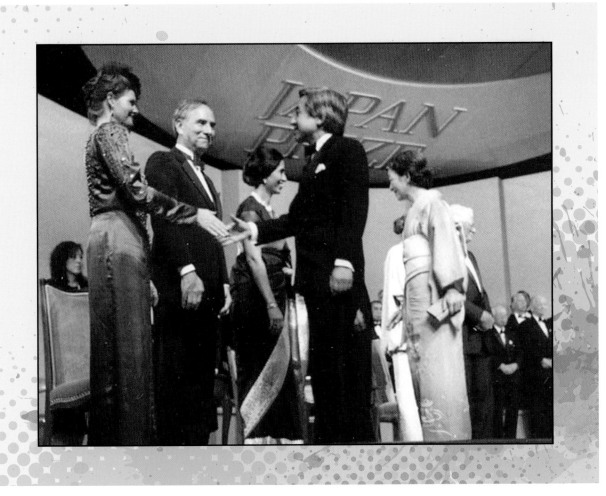

Ted received the Japan Prize in 1987. His wife, Kathleen, shakes hands with Emperor Akihito of Japan as Ted looks on.

TIMELINE

1927—Born in Los Angeles, California, on July 11.

1928—Family moves to Denver, Colorado.

1939—Becomes assistant in one-man radio shop.

1943—Family moves to Morristown, New Jersey.

1944—Joins Navy; designs test equipment for military radio tubes.

1949—Graduates with bachelor of science in engineering from University of Colorado; studies at Columbia University.

1951—Earns master of science degree in engineering from Stanford University, California.

1955—Earns Ph.D. in physics from Stanford University.

1956—Joins Hughes Aircraft Company's research laboratory, Culver City, California.

1960—In April, experts tell him that his work on a ruby laser is foolish; one month later, on May 16, he demonstrates the world's first working laser.

1962—Founds Korad Company to produce ruby lasers.

1968—Founds Maiman Associates to search out and invest in science-based businesses.

1976—Becomes vice president of TRW, an aircraft company, heading a major research organization.

1984—Is elected to National Inventors Hall of Fame; moves to Vancouver, Canada.

2007—Dies in Vancouver on May 5.

YOU BE THE INVENTOR!

So you want to be an inventor? You can do it! First, you need a terrific idea.

Got a problem? No problem!

Many inventions begin when someone thinks of a great solution to a problem. One cold day in 1994, 10-year-old K.K. Gregory was building a snow fort. Soon, she had snow between her mittens and her coat sleeve. Her wrists were cold and wet. She found some scraps of fabric around the house, and used them to make a tube that would fit around her wrist. She cut a thumbhole in the tube to

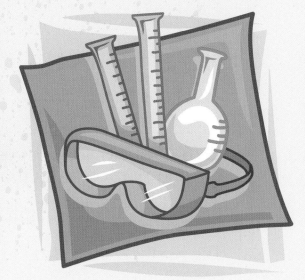

make a kind of fingerless glove, and called it a "Wristie." Wearing mittens over her new invention, her wrists stayed nice and warm when she played outside. Today, the Wristie business is booming.

Now it's your turn. Maybe, like K.K. Gregory, you have an idea for something new that would make your life better or easier. Perhaps you can think of a way improve an everyday item. Twelve year-old Becky Schroeder became the youngest female ever to receive a U.S. patent after she invented a glow-in-the dark clipboard that allowed people to write in the dark. Do you like to play sports or board games? James Naismith, inspired by a game he used to play as a boy, invented a new game he called basketball.

Let your imagination run wild. You never know where it will take you.

Research it!

Okay, you have a terrific idea for an invention. Now what?

First, you'll want to make sure that nobody else has thought of your idea. You wouldn't want to spend hours developing your new invention, only to find that someone else beat you to it. Google Patents can help you find out whether your idea is original.

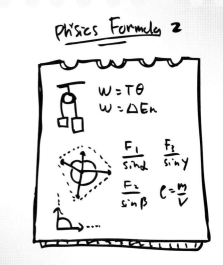

Bring it to life!

If no one else has thought of your idea, congratulations! Write it down in a logbook or journal. Write the date and your initials for every entry you make. If you file a patent for your

invention later, this will help you prove that you were the first person to think of it. The most important thing about this logbook is that pages cannot be added or subtracted. You can buy a bound notebook at any office supply store.

Draw several different pictures of your invention in your logbook. Try sketching views from above, below, and to the side. Show how big each part of your invention should be.

Build a model. Don't be discouraged if it doesn't work at first. You may have to experiment with different designs and materials. That's part of the fun! Take pictures of everything, and tape them into your logbook.

Try your invention out on your friends and family. If they have any suggestions to make it better, build another model. Perfect your invention, and give it a clever name.

Patent it!

Do you want to sell your invention? You'll want to apply for a patent. Holding a patent to your invention means that no one else can make, use, or sell your invention in the U.S. without your permission. It prevents others from making money off of your idea. You will definitely need an adult to help you apply for a patent. It can be a complicated and expensive process. But if you think that people will want to buy your invention, it is well worth it.

WORDS TO KNOW

engineering—Using math and physics to design and build new things.

laboratory—A place to do scientific experiments.

laser—An instrument that makes a very narrow and very strong beam of light. Lasers can be used to cut hard material, remove diseased body tissue, and more.

Ph.D.—The highest degree a student can earn from a university. It means doctor of philosophy.

physics—The science of materials and energy and how they act together.

radar—Radio waves used to find objects. Radar is use by the military to find enemy boats and airplanes.

ruby—A precious pink or red natural stone often used in jewelry. Rubies can also be made in laboratories and used for science.

university—A place where people go to learn after graduating from high school.

watt—In physics, a unit to measure how powerful something is.

LEARN MORE

Books

Clements, Gillian. *The Picture History of Great Inventors.* London: Frances Lincoln, 2005.

Connolly, Sean. *The Book of Potentially Catastrophic Science: 50 Experiments for Daring Young Scientists.* New York: Workman Publishing Company, 2010.

Hibbert, Claire. *Green Lantern's Book of Great Inventions.* New York: DK Readers, 2005.

Macaulay, David. *The New Way Things Work.* Boston: Houghton Mifflin Co., 1998.

Sadler, Wendy. *Light: Look Out!* Chicago: Raintree, 2006.

LEARN MORE

Internet Addresses

To find out more about Theodore Maiman, inventions, and lasers, check out these Web sites:

NASA's The Space Place: What is a laser?
<http://spaceplace.nasa.gov/laser/redirected/>

Britannica Kids: Theodore Harold Maiman
<http://kids.britannica.com/comptons/article-9328893>

If you want to learn more about becoming an inventor, check out these Web sites:

Inventnow.org
<http://www.inventnow.org/>

Inventive Kids
<http://www.inventivekids.com/>

The U.S. Patent and Trademark Office For Kids
<http://www.uspto.gov/kids/>

INDEX